A NEW LOOK AT OLD CLITHEROE

A New Look
at Old Clitheroe

Changes in the Eighteenth
and Nineteenth Centuries

Robert O. Jones

Carnegie Publishing, 1997

© R. O. Jones, 1997

First published in 1997 by
Carnegie Publishing Ltd,
18 Maynard Street, Preston PR2 2AL

ISBN 1–85936–048–3

Typeset in Monotype Fournier by
Carnegie Publishing, 18 Maynard St, Preston

Printed and bound by
Redwood Books, Trowbridge, Wilts

Contents

Illustrations

Introduction

I T is almost sixty years since Arthur Langshaw published his first writings about his adopted town, beginning with a *Child's History of Clitheroe* in 1938. This book is by way of a 'Thank you' to him by another incomer. My approach is quite different but it will, I hope, prove of interest to the residents of Clitheroe and the Ribble Valley as we approach the 21st century.

In the year 2001 the census is very likely to show Clitheroe to have a population exceeding 14,000 for the first time.

I have concentrated on some aspects of the town history during the eighteenth and nineteenth centuries partly because of the M. Oddie 1781 sketch which Arthur Langshaw never saw. Many hundreds of Clitheroe residents made a contribution to ensure this sketch returned to the town and these essays are also written as an appreciation of their interest and efforts.

Robert O. Jones

True or False

THE *Victoria County History* of Lancashire, published, rather ironically, eleven years after the Queen's death, is by any standards a lengthy work. It comprises eight volumes, each several hundred pages long. In volume six on page 360 the following words are found:

'The story of Clitheroe is of little interest.'

The purpose of the essays in this book is to deny the charge but, in all fairness, attention should be given to points which may seem to justify the statement. After all, a Yorkshireman will not easily praise or defend Lancashire history, traditions or ways unless he is convinced of the case.

◻ THE CASTLE or more correctly the Norman Keep has not played a significant part in the history of England nor, as many would argue, in the lives of Clitheronians during the last thousand years. In the twentieth century the image of the Keep has understandably been used, to good effect, to promote the economy of the town, mainly as a tourist attraction. Television pictures from time to time provide the town with good publicity on a county and national scale.

◻ THE CHURCH. As Clitheroe uses its Keep so East Anglian and Cotswolds towns and villages portray to good advantage the wonderful architecture of their 'wool' churches. Our late medieval church, in use until 1828, did in its own way reflect the simple, dour, hard, tough, no-nonsense northern life familiar to many. Until the eighteenth century Lancashire was one of the most sparsely populated and economically poor counties in the country and Clitheroe mirrored this.

◻ POPULATION. The fact that the population of Clitheroe took some seven hundred years from Norman times until the 1780s to rise from three hundred to one thousand hardly indicates the significant development of an important settlement. The last twenty years of the eighteenth century saw the population

St. Mary's, Clitheroe, from the early 1400s until 1828. A previous church had stood on this site from c. 1122.

4

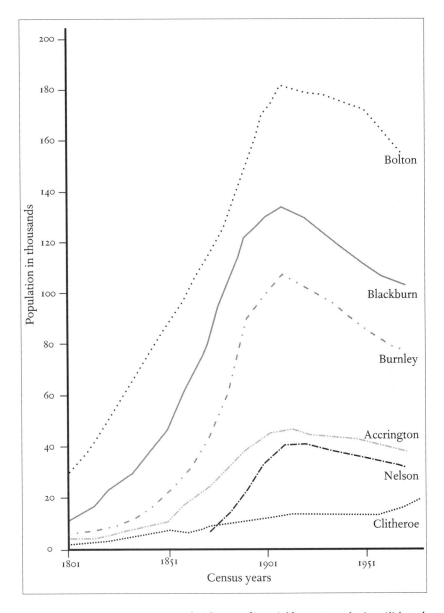

Population graph, Clitheroe compared with some of its neighbours. It emphasises Clitheroe's very different development compared with other Lancashire towns.

increase dramatically, relatively speaking, by around four hundred – the result of what, in general terms, we call the industrial revolution. Even in this context Clitheroe in the nineteenth century seemed only marginally involved in the most important century in the economic, social and political history of Lancashire. A look at the population statistics of that century show Clitheroe in a very different light compared with its neighbours Accrington, Nelson, Burnley, Blackburn and Bolton. It developed – thank goodness say many – in a very different way from those communities.

¤ PROSPERITY. The attractive picture drawn in words, paintings and photographs of The Swan, Starkie Arms and White Lion i.e. 'Clitheroe in its Coaching Days' needs to be examined with care. Coaching played a very minor part in its history. The three inns, as we know them, were all re(built) in the late 1830s. The three examples quoted below give a more realistic picture of Clitheroe's economic position in the late eighteenth century and early nineteenth century:

¤ 1792. A visitor describes The Swan, "A poor ale house received us. My bed chamber was very wretched with an old broken deal door which I fortified with chains; and through which every passenger in the house might see me in bed."

¤ 1826. Steward at the castle to the new Headmaster: "Whilst your home is arranged if you will make the Castle your home the old woman there will do what she can for you, and she will make you as comfortable (Bed and Board) as you will be at either inn."

¤ 1831. Parliamentary Boundary Commission. "The condition of the town is poor, and within it there are very few houses of any size or description that present an appearance of opulence or comfort."

I have listed several examples which indicate that Clitheroe's long history has not been a remarkable one. However, that certainly is not the same as suggesting that its story is of little interest. Indeed, the facts seeking to play down the importance of the town are in themselves revealing.

Arthur Langshaw must surely rank as a local historian of great importance. Very few towns will have had their day-to-day story unfolded in such a remarkable way. He found the story of Clitheroe to be a fascinating one. He was right. The Victorian County History quote is wrong.

6

Two Half Sisters

MUCH of the interest in Clitheroe's eighteenth- and nineteenth-century story is due to the actions of two women in the middle of the sixteenth century.

Ruthless, determined, stubborn – full of guile and ability – each took one decisive action which had a continuing influence on Clitheroe's history. Mary Tudor was the older one, Elizabeth Tudor the younger. Many historians would argue that the Tudors were the most successful and talented family to rule England, as they did, between 1485 and 1603. Their grandfather Henry VII united the feuding families of York and Lancaster after defeating Richard III at Bosworth. Henry VIII, greatly involved with the political and religious quarrel with Rome, is perhaps best known simply because he had six wives.

Mary reigned from 1553 to 1558. In 1554 she founded Clitheroe Royal Grammar School. Why? Two reasons suggest themselves for her favourable reception of a petition for such a school.

There is evidence that a school of some kind had existed in the town as far back as the end of the thirteenth century. A school was certainly functioning in 1473 and whilst there may have been

Elizabeth I

7

Mary I

periods when the school was not operating, pupils were from time to time taught by priests, most probably in the parish church. This school ceased to exist after the Reformation and the Dissolution of the Monastaries coupled with the suppression of chantries between 1547 and 1553.

Mary was always an adherent of the old pre-Reformation church whose leader was the Pope in Rome. She may well have been keen to restart the school. In addition she would be aware that Lancashire remained a county loyal to the pre-Reformation Church and she may well have been minded to say 'Thank you' to the county by the founding of a free grammar school. Funds to support the school came, at first, from the rent of lands in the Skipton area.

Four years later Elizabeth, aged 25 years, granted Clitheroe the right to elect two members of parliament. Why? Elizabeth, certainly in the early years of her reign, walked a tightrope between the old Church and the newly established Church of England. She sought to ensure that the majority of members of parliament were loyal – but not over zealous – to the Church of England. She did not like extreme Roman Catholics nor extreme Protestants. Elizabeth used a privilege (which did not end until the reign of Charles II) of making townships into parliamentary boroughs. During her reign she gave Cornwall thirty M.P.s, bringing its total to 44, the highest of any county. This situation remained until the Reform Act of 1832.

The Honour of Clitheroe belonged to the Crown between 1399 and 1661. It was easy for Elizabeth to give the town representation. Voting rights depended largely upon the ownership of burgage property within the borough. All Tudor monarchs used this method of ensuring control of Parliament, i.e. M.P. place-men, often with no local connections, supported Crown policy. Between 1485 and 1603 the number of M.P.s rose from 298 to 443.

Two Eighteenth-century Families

IT is time to examine some of the events which occurred in the eighteenth and nineteenth centuries – to look in more detail at some of the families and individuals involved. We can begin with a particular day, Boxing Day 1743.

A young man in his early twenties was riding from Clitheroe to Bolton by Bowland. It was his wedding day. He was to marry a young widow – Ann Walker. Tradition has it that he found time during this ride to join the Bolton by Bowland Boxing Day hunt yet still arrive in time for the wedding. His name – James King, the newly appointed Vicar of Clitheroe.

While he was getting married another young couple were spending Christmas at their home – the original Alleys house – then very much past its former glory. This original house was on the site of the recently demolished (1994) St Denys Home on Pimlico Road. William Oddie was the young husband; his wife prior to marriage had been Jane Lister, a sister of the Gisburn landowner.

The Kings eventually had a family of nine children, two of whom died in infancy or childhood. They were fortunate. The Oddies had fourteen children, only seven of whom reached adulthood.

Looking through the Clitheroe Parish Church registers it is possible to highlight trends in births, marriages and deaths which occurred over the period 1740 to 1800. The year 1750 was perhaps the most difficult personally for the King and Oddie families as well as other families in the town.

Fifty-four people – many of them infants died during that year, most of them in the last three months of 1750. James King and his wife lost a daughter, 21 months; the Oddies lost two infants within two months and another family buried three children on 24th November 1750. Over the ten-year period 1740–50 the average death rate was 25, i.e. 25 people died in a year. Two other years where the number dying greatly exceeded the ten-year average

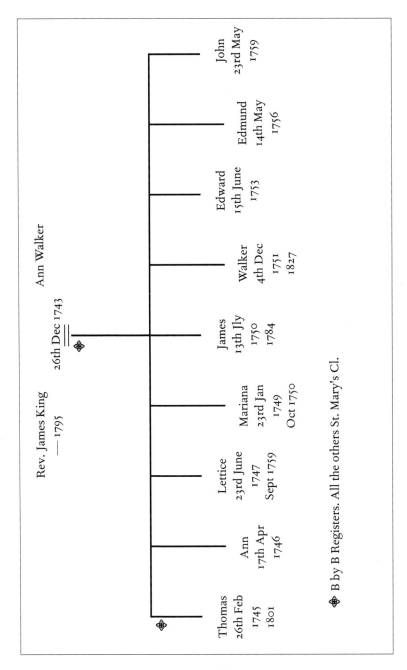

Rev. James King   Ann Walker

— 1795

26th Dec 1743

Thomas
26th Feb
1745
1801

Ann
17th Apr
1746

Lettice
23rd June
1747
Sept 1759

Mariana
23rd Jan
1749
Oct 1750

James
13th Jly
1750
1784

Walker
4th Dec
1751
1827

Edward
15th June
1753

Edmund
14th May
1756

John
23rd May
1759

✦ B by B Registers. All the others St. Mary's Cl.

The King Family Tree

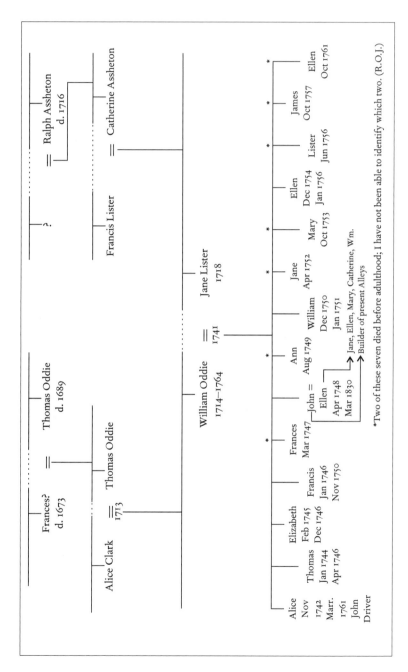

The Oddie Family Tree

were 1756 and 1793. There is no written evidence pinpointing the reason for these high death rates. The registers show that between 1780 and 1800 the average death rate rose significantly, probably reflecting an increased population as Low Moor and Primrose mills launched the town into the industrial revolution. Over the same period there is a marked increase in the number of marriages.

James King was officially associated with Clitheroe from 1743 to 1775 although it would seem that after 1772 his presence in the town was rare. He lived in a property which stood on the site of the Yorkshire Bank on the corner of King Lane and the Market Place (1996). After 1775 until 1921 an inn with several names stood on this site, the best known, The Brownlow Arms, playing a full role in Clitheroe's social and economic development. During the nineteenth century and until about 1914 the stables for the Brownlow Arms were on land on the south side of King Lane. Since that time the site has been home to a concert hall, a cinema and in the 1960s became the first supermarket in the town – Hillards. By the 1990s the site had retirement homes – proof that, like it or not, a town must adapt to changing times.

From 1772 King was Vicar of Guildford; in 1774 he was a Canon of Windsor; by 1776 he was Dean of Raphoe, County Donegal, and also Chaplain to the House of Commons. Several of his sons held high office. People in Clitheroe remember best Captain James King R.N. (1750–1784) who sailed with Captain Cook on his last voyage. One son was Prependary of Canterbury Cathedral and Chancellor at Lincoln; another became Bishop of Rochester; another Vice Chancellor of the Duchy of Lancaster and yet another an Under Secretary of State in several governments.

How did a Clitheroe clergyman and his sons suddenly move into such elevated circles? Late eighteenth-century England was noted for patronage in both State and Church. Certain favoured clergy held several livings at once and often did not visit the places where they held posts. It may just be possible the King family became fortunate in this respect though I have not researched this field.

Of the seven surviving children of William and Jane Oddie the one we know most about is a son, John. He was born in 1747 and lived to be 82 years old. He has a part to play in a later essay in this book. Suffice to say at the moment that he was the builder of the present Alleys (though he called

13

it Spring Gardens). Built probably in the 1780s it was occupied by his children until the last one died in 1877. She was Jane and also lived until the age of 82 years. Her grandfather, William, had died in 1764 aged 50 years. His widow, Jane – mother of the fourteen children – was still alive in Colne in 1777.

Disaster and Triumph

D URING the first two hundred years of its existence Clitheroe Grammar School had, to say the least, some interesting characters as headmasters. The youngest, aged nineteen, held the post for two years. John Glazebrook was tried for murder at Lancaster. Fortunately he was acquitted though he left Clitheroe soon after. At one stage a headmaster was called upon to 'hold the fort' for a second time. He was eighty years old and did not last long.

Most of the appointments went to young men in their early twenties, some, but not all took holy orders. Early death was not unusual and it is likely some very promising people did not live long enough to make a lasting impression. A school in Appleby, Cumbria, perhaps holds the record for the longest serving head. During the eighteenth century one person held the post for fifty-eight years until his death at the age of eighty-one!

Twenty-five year old Matthew Sedgewick arrived in 1750 and stayed for twenty-four years. He certainly made an impression – the wrong one, as the extracts below show. He was a disaster! Once the governors of the school had chosen their head his licence to teach came from the Bishop of Chester and only he could revoke it. The governors tried but Sedgewick must have been very tenacious. He it was who in his last two years at Clitheroe also stood in for James King who had moved to Guildford.

In 1760 the governors asked for a formal review of his conduct. In a letter to the Bishop they alleged:

> that Mr. Sedgwick had for the space of five or six years last been very careless and negligent in his duty as Schoolmaster, kept very loose company, followed idle diversions in no way consistent with a man of his cloathing, frequently quarrelling, fighting in publick upon challengers and with people of low rank, and guilty of many other vices tending to immorality:

that for upwards of eighteen months last past he Mr. Sedgwick had not one Scholar and, tho the Usher or undermaster had a great number and rather more than he could well take care of, that Mr. Sedgwick never gave him any assistance.

They went on to assert that they had frequently admonished and reprimanded him over his conduct but without the least success.

The Bishop did not support the petition. He spoke to Sedgewick who promised to make more effort. A second petition in 1772 caused Sedgewick to write a letter of resignation which was not acted upon until 1774 when one of the governors again wrote to the Bishop as follows:

He has most shamefully neglected His School, and still continues to do so, even now. He very rarely goes into it before 10 and sometimes 11 o'clock in ye mornings, stays about half an Hour or an Hour, and perhaps repeats ye same abt 4 o'clock in ye afternoon, but sometimes never goes there at all. He has often declared that He cannot bear ye attendance, let what will be ye consequence. The Master's standing salary is £40 and ye Usher's £30 a year. The Revenues are now in a good deal increased, which we are to apply in augmenting these salaries, in repairs, and in assisting young men at ye University, but this he has prevented during His time for He never has had ye credit to send one there tho' he has been Master above 20 years, whereas scarce a year pass'd without some being sent there by all ye former Masters that can be remember'd. We hope for yr Ldsp's assent to his resignation.

The Bishop – a recently appointed one – agreed that Matthew Sedgewick would have to go. He went. Throughout this difficult time for the school, the usher or second master Ephraim Garthwaite was its mainstay. Appointed in 1728 he remained in post until his death in 1775. It would have been Garthwaite who had most to do with the education given to the sons of the Rev. James King and the sons of William and Jane Oddie.

Thomas Wilson arrived on the scene in 1775. He combined the post of Vicar and headmaster for thirty-eight years. Two for the price of one, in the supermarket jargon of 1996, though in reality he was paid for both responsibilities. He was, undoubtedly, the most successful headmaster and vicar Clitheroe had in the eighteenth century.

In one respect he followed the footsteps of Rev. James King. Thomas

Wilson also rode out to Bolton by Bowland in 1775 to marry a widow, Susanna Howell. Her first husband had been Rector of Bolton by Bowland. She was aged 44 and already had three teenage children. As a young girl she had been brought up as a Quaker. There were no children following this marriage and Susanna died in 1804 and was buried at Bolton by Bowland.

Within six years of coming to Clitheroe Wilson had the wholehearted support of the governors in his desire to rebuild the school. During his headship numbers on roll rose to more than 100, the highest in the lifetime of the school. Most of the pupils were sons of the local gentry and came from as far afield as Blackburn, Burnley and Colne. Some of the pupils boarded with Wilson, others were scattered about the town in various lodgings. The Old Boys Association had its beginnings in the late 1780s, a tribute to the success of and regard in which Wilson was held.

Not for more than one hundred years after 1813 did the school again have one hundred pupils. Indeed, between the years 1818 and 1840 numbers on roll varied between one and twenty. In the second half of the nineteenth century numbers ranged from twenty-three to sixty-five (38 day pupils, 27 boarders). In 1900 there were forty on roll.

The school had little impact on the development of nineteenth-century Clitheroe, as the small number of pupils indicates. During the twentieth century, particularly the second half, the school is, once again, held in high esteem within the whole of the Ribble Valley and beyond. Thomas Wilson would have been proud of his school. He still keeps an alert eye on the town! His portrait gazes down on those who attend concerts and lectures in the Library meeting room – previously the Clitheroe borough council chamber, between 1822 and 1974.

A Family Quarrel

REFERENCE has already been made to the parliamentary representation granted by Queen Elizabeth. In the early eighteenth century the then male line of the Asshetons of Downham died. His two daughters were married, one to a Lister of Gisburn the other into the Curzon family.

These two families as the major landowners of burgage property within Clitheroe each sent a representative from their families or another nominee to parliament between 1727 and 1780. There were no elections. This arrangement lasted through twelve opportunities when voting could have been possible.

A family quarrel in 1780 upset the cosy arrangement. There were three candidates – all Tories. Thomas Lister supported the idea of his brother in law – John Parker of Browsholme Hall – becoming an M.P. rather than Assheton Curzon.

The voting figures were:

Thomas Lister	33
John Parker	31
Assheton Curzon	17

A dispute flared up about who owned particular burgage land and houses and therefore who had the rights to certain votes. Thomas Lister appointed M. Oddie, surveyor, to draw a town plan indicating ownership. He was assisted by another Oddie – no relation. This was the John Oddie mentioned earlier (1747–1830). He acted as Lister's agent in Clitheroe. His mother Jane was an aunt of Thomas Lister and so Lister and John Oddie were cousins. The fact that the Oddie name occurs twice adds further complication and interest, which is explained in detail later.

Had this family quarrel not happened the 1781 map of Clitheroe would not have been drawn. The map itself is not unlike Lang's 1766 map of the town – the earliest known one.

The most interesting feature of Matthew Oddie's map – not shown on Lang's – is a building in the middle of Castle Street between the Starkie Arms and Penthouse Pottery (1996). This medieval penthouse consisted of a ground floor, open to the elements, with stone pillars, four or perhaps more supporting an upper room where borough business was conducted before the building of the first Moot Hall around 1610 – the site of the present library. By 1784 the penthouse which had very likely been in a ruined state for many years had disappeared. Written records indicate a small sum of money was paid for its demolition. The penthouse probably dated from the fourteenth century.

As far as local historians are concerned family quarrels are sometimes a blessing in disguise. The M. Oddie sketch of the castle, dated 1781, returned to Clitheroe in February 1995, and now in the library, was an additional bonus. The town gained a map and a picture of the mid eighteenth-century castle. Lang's map of 1766 shows the new layout of the castle grounds, thus helping to pinpoint that the mansion house was built between 1723 and 1766 – perhaps around 1750. No exact information has come to light.

A Mystery

Despite a considerable amount of research, Matthew Oddie's background is proving difficult to establish. There appears to be nothing in the way of information in Clitheroe records. Records at Colne refer to two people of that name – both Quakers. A document dated 1820 lists information about M. Oddie, surveyor. Examination of this at Lancashire Record Office states:

Ref D C W Matthew Oddie 1820

"Mrs Satterthwaite, a widow, the lawful sister and next of kin and administrix of all and singular the goods and chattels and credits of Matthew Oddie late of the town and parish of Colne in the County of Lancashire, deceased a bachelor without parent or brother.

Ann Satterthwaite, Quaker, made the solemn affirmation instead of the usual oath. Estate and effects under the value of £200. The intestate died 4 May 1792."

The directory of Land Surveyors gives the earliest and latest known work of M. Oddie as 1770 to 1794. Although M. Oddie died in 1792 it can be reasonably argued that some of his work was published in 1794 after his death. The discrepancy in dates may not be vital. There is no reference to his age on death.

The Quaker link is maintained in the directory of Land Surveyors. It suggests that Matthew Oddie was a pupil of William Fairbank, 1730–1790, himself a Quaker and like his father a surveyor and schoolmaster.

Examination of Quaker records in the Marsden area (Colne) does not show the death of a Matthew Oddie in 1792. It does show someone of that name born in 1754 and one who died in 1798 at the age of 44 years – very likely to be the same person. There is no indication of occupation. Many of the Quaker Oddies listed appeared to be shoemakers or cloggers. The Oddie who died in 1798 was married. His wife's death is the next recorded entry in 1799.

Why should there be so much concern on my part to find definite proof? Another Oddie family exists – a Clitheroe one – prominent in the eighteenth century and until 1877. There may have been an M. Oddie aged about 28 in 1781, I had hoped to prove that it was this Oddie who drew the sketch. So far I have not been successful. For this person to have drawn the sketch would be like putting the icing on the cake, not because they lived in Clitheroe but because M. Oddie was a woman.

She was one of the large family mentioned earlier, half of whom died in infancy. Her brother John built the present Alleys – Pimlico Road. Two sisters married Clitheroe men. Of Mary Oddie I can find no records of marriage or death, though her birth is listed in the church records. The Oddie family was linked by marriage to the landowners and local gentry – Listers of Gisburn and Parkers of Browsholme who owned the sketch for over 200 years.

For many years it has been accepted that M. Oddie, who drew the town plan of Clitheroe in 1781, was a Matthew Oddie. At the moment it seems that whoever drew the town plan also drew the sketch. Is it just possible that a Matthew drew the plan and Mary the sketch. Could she have done both? Unlikely, but a wonderful fairytale ending if someone can prove it. After all, her brother John was agent to the Lister family who caused the map to be drawn following a family dispute over the ownership of land, property and voting rights in Clitheroe.

The 'New' Castle

Now that the Oddie castle sketch (1781) is on permanent view for all to enjoy at Clitheroe Library, it is important to reflect on its significance. It is the most accurate and detailed drawing of the castle area attempted during the eighteenth century. There is a need to reassess what has been written about the castle and grounds over the last 200 years.

We begin by considering what is missing from the sketch. The chapel and gatehouse have gone. This confirms what various sources have suggested.

Castle sketch, M. Oddie 1781. Original found, by author, at Gargrave, Nov. 1994. Now in Clitheroe Library after being bought by public subscription Feb. 1995

An engraving ordered by Act of Parliament and drawn by George Vertue in 1753, it appears to be a copy of an earlier drawing and not an actual representation of the castle at the time. A well-known engraving but not very informative. R.O.J.

Baines *History of Lancashire*, 1868 and *Victoria County History*, 1911, are examples of publications which make reference to the slighting and dismantling of the castle after the Civil War ended in 1649. There is no definite evidence if, when or how the gatehouse and chapel disappeared, nor whether any serious work was done to make the castle useless as a fortification. It is generally accepted that any materials lying about in the chapel or gatehouse areas may have been used in eighteenth-century reconstruction.

Perhaps we should argue the case for the disappearance of the chapel from another angle. Remember that the Honour of Clitheroe belonged to the Crown from 1399 to 1661, the longest continued direct ownership in the history of the Honour.

The Chapel had links with Whalley Abbey. It was of little importance to the people of Clitheroe; they had their own church, St Mary's. The castle and its grounds did not become part of the borough until 1895. As late as the 1891 census the castle was listed separately (extra parochial) with some 10 or 12 people living there – the Steward's family and servants.

How far would the chapel have been cared for after the Dissolution of the Monasteries in the reign of Henry VIII? How far would Elizabeth I, well known for keeping a tight control of the purse strings, be worried about a late sixteenth-century report on the state of the castle indicating money was required for repairs? It can be argued with some conviction that the gatehouse, chapel and keep gradually crumbled away through neglect. Small sums were spent from time to time but not much!

The present museum and sound archive buildings were built in the eighteenth century, probably on the site of earlier buildings. The museum, called the castle or mansion, provided a home and offices for the Steward of the Honour of Clitheroe. The sound archive building was a court house. Whoever held the Honour was holding a valuable asset. It comprised the Hundred of Blackburn, part of the Hundred of Salford together with property in the Forest of Bowland – part of Yorkshire.

There is no precise proof about when the extensive renovation took place. A. Langshaw suggests 1723, though the plans and drawings upon which the evidence is based are quite different from what was built. The Buck drawing of 1727 – a very romantic and stylised sketch – dedicated to John, Duke of Montague who held the Honour, shows no castle building as Oddie's sketch shows it. It can be argued that, had the Duke done all this work prior to 1727 the artists would have had the sense to show it or mention the fact in their caption.

The Duke did not die until 1749 when, for more than 75 years, the Honour was in the hands of the female side of the family. There are no stewards' records of costs, no accounts from builders, carpenters or other workers. Such vital evidence may turn up in the future. For the time being we must settle for sources which suggest that the middle years of the century saw the renovation.

We should consider briefly some of the other fairly well-known pictures of the castle drawn in the eighteenth and nineteenth centuries. Buck's picture, already mentioned, needs looking at once more. The faulty perspective of the keep with Pendle Hill, the positioning of the town, the fact that it is a view from the west and not south as stated are vital points which prevent us from accepting it as a serious representation of what the castle looked like in 1727.

George Vertue's drawing of 1753, though officially undertaken for parliament, is halfway between a plan and sketch. Detail is sparse and it is recognised as being based on a late sixteenth-century drawing, perhaps done for Elizabeth I.

An engraving, sometimes dated 1775, sometimes 1784, shows the keep and grounds from a considerable distance and therefore without much detail. Turner's sketch of 1799 from Edisford Bridge and Weld's 1835 watercolour are both distant views.

We now consider various features shown in the Oddie sketch. Foremost amongst these are the two pillars on the site where the gatehouse or its ruins stood for some 600 years. When next you walk up the driveway, notice how these pillars are out of line with the present driveway. They remain at their original angle when the roadway, very steep, came directly from Castle Street, i.e. from the narrow road at the back of Steele's, solicitors. If you walk along that back way you can see in the high wall a stone gatepost which marks how the road went until the longer more gentle slope was made in the late 1830s. If you walk still further along, past several garages and as far as you can go, the remains of the curved wall below the pillars can still be seen.

Note the buttresses at either end of the castle or mansion house. They are still there. Oddie drew the correct number of windows and their correct shape. Missing, of course, is the present porchway into the museum. That was a Victorian addition, as was the building we now see sandwiched between the

Nath. & Sam. Buck 1727
A fairy tale picture! R.O.J.

26

courthouse and the stables. No 'Oliver Cromwell' gaping hole in the keep –
another Clitheroe legend bites the dust?! There are very definite signs of
crumbling masonry showing at the south-east corner of the keep.

Note also a roofless barn at the bottom right-hand side as well as three or
four thatched buildings. A number of Clitheroe buildings had thatched roofs
well into the nineteenth century. The Victoria Hotel, then known as Calf's
Head, had a thatched roof until rebuilt in the 1850s. In 1824 Margaret Hyde
let the White Horse in Church Street to Francis Silverwood and agreed to
provide spelks and straw for thatching and to pay the thatcher's wages.

The Watershed, 1781–1782

DURING the early paragraphs of this essay the reader is invited to assume the role of Captain James King, R.N. (1750–1784). Born in Clitheroe, the son of the Rev. James King, he left the town at the age of twelve for a career in the Royal Navy. Locally he is remembered for his association with Captain James Cook and his last voyage to Australia.

Had he returned to his home town in 1781 and viewed it from the castle keep he would have found it unchanged from his childhood days. Looking down, he would have pondered on an unremarkable town/village, i.e. the small built up area.

Where the present Starkie Arms stands (built in the 1830s) were the remains of an old inn – the Rose and Crown – a name often associated with Tudor times. In the street close by were the remains of the medieval penthouse, its importance long gone since the first Moot Hall was built in the early seventeenth century. Much of the property would have had thatched roofing. King may have spotted some activity in the churchyard where workmen were rebuilding his old school.

Had he returned, with his naval telescope, in 1782 he may have been astonished to see a new large building about a mile from the Castle. This would have been the first Low Moor mill; Clitheroe had belatedly joined the rest of Lancashire. The industrial revolution had arrived. Thomas Wilson, vicar and headmaster 1775–1813 was to see many changes before his death. He took a close interest in all that was happening.

An interesting facet of local history, in any part of the country, is the way a particular event or development has unforseen consequences for the future. Low Moor mill provides an excellent example of this. The building of the weir just below Waddow Hall caused the river to deepen and widen. The immediate effect is well documented. It became difficult to cross the ford at Brungerley and the hipping stones often became submerged. In 1784 five extra

Brungerley Bridge, built 1816

hipping stones were put into the river bed on the Clitheroe side. This was not a satisfactory solution, nor was the second attempt to solve the problem. A wooden bridge with foundations in the hipping stones lasted from about 1800 until the stone bridge was built in 1816.

A very important social development in Clitheroe's history began in 1876, ninety-four years after the weir was built. Eli Tucker, a tenant in the cottages at Brungerley, began to hire boats for rowing on the river. A thriving business by Tucker and his sons was maintained into the 1930s. Hundreds of cotton workers from neighbouring towns came by train for a day out during bank holidays and weekends. Easter weekend saw the opening of the boating season.

The 1927 Midland Railway Guide still drew attention to this tourist attraction. Eli Tucker was born in Somerset and came to Waddington as a young man working as a groom and coachman. He was born in 1841 and died at the age of eighty-five. Tucker Hill is the name given to one of the roads on the 1990s' housing development near to Brungerley Park. This is an excellent example of what local history is all about – linking the past with the present. In 1992 an exceptionally dry August coupled with river authority work at the

This page and following: *August 1992. Brungerley Hippings.*

The 5 extra Hipping stones put in place in 1784 – written records give details

weir so lowered the level of the river that the five 1784 hipping stones were seen for the first time in almost two hundred years. Photographs were taken! The other major mill, opened in 1787, was Primrose, followed by a succession of smaller ones: 1797 Upbrooks and Shaw Bridge known as 'Standstill' and 'Puff and Dart'. Then came Brewery Mill, 1808, rebuilt in 1837 as Claremont Mill. 1788 also saw the final Enclosure Act for common land within the township of Clitheroe. Methodist and R.C. chapels were built in 1797, a congregational one in 1815. By 1809 Moor Lane provided a direct route into the town centre from Primrose Bridge and Whalley. In the 1820s Clitheroe rebuilt its Moot Hall, the new building being known as the Town Hall, its Parish Church and developed York Street and the new road to Chatburn.

Further mills were developed by the side of Mearley Brook – a much more important stream than the Ribble as far as the economic development of the cotton trade was concerned. Two other major public buildings opened in 1839: St James Church and the National School in Moor Lane where Arthur Langshaw was head between 1908 and its closure in 1932.

In a book written in the 1920s H. V. Morton used the sentence "Clitheroe is half in fairyland and half in Lancashire." Such a sentence helped to promote Clitheroe as a tourist area before the Second World War. The importance of tourism in the area has continued ever since.

Two factors, or their absence, determined Clitheroe's different development compared with other cotton towns. The absence of coalfields and to a lesser extent the fact that the Leeds and Liverpool Canal development did not follow its early planned routes enabled Clitheroe to remain a market town set in the attractive surroundings of the Ribble Valley. Certainly the cotton industry was important but the economy of the town remained more balanced and diverse than that of many cotton towns. King Cotton in Lancashire, yes. Perhaps it was only Prince Cotton in Clitheroe.

This chapter ends as it began, on an imaginary note. It assumes the existence of *The Clitheroe Advertiser and Times* and its lively feature of a reader's letter page in 1781. This is linked with late twentieth-century concern of local communities for the environment, thus resulting in the following letter.

Vandalism in the R.V. 1781

Dear Sir

I have been given a copy of a secret document which will change the nature of the valley and the town.

I understand that negotiations are taking place which will allow a cotton mill to be built on the banks of the River Ribble near Edisford Bridge. If finally approved Thomas Weddall, the owner of Waddow Hall will give permission for a weir to be built across the river in order to allow a head of water to be channelled through to the proposed site. The wording of the proposed agreement is as follows:- 'liberty to erect, make or construct all other such cauls, dams, sluices and reservoirs as might be necessary'.

Our beautiful valley is to be ruined. As the river is deepened by the building of a weir it will become impossible to use the hipping stones at Brungerley and the water will be too deep for carts and horses to cross the ford.

Perhaps even worse is the fact that there will be very limited employment for local people. I understand from contacts in Manchester, Bolton, Preston and Blackburn that many of the labourers to operate this dark satanic mill are to be orphan children and beggars from London.

If this proposal goes through I predict that within fifty years Mearley Brook will have cotton mills on its banks and pollution will make life unbearable. Rumours of the invention of a steam engine by James Watt being used to power cotton looms will make pollution worse. There will be huge chimneys belching out smoke into the atmosphere.

Disgusted, Clitheroe.

Environmental concerns, late twentieth-century seen through eighteenth-century eyes

The Keep – Saved
by an Unknown Artist? 1848

IN 1848 two detailed sketches of Clitheroe Castle Keep were made. The artist is unknown. The date August 1848 is on the originals and the size of the unframed drawings is 10¼ ins × 14¼ ins.

The originals were seen in July 1995 by a group of local historians checking, under the supervision of county museum staff, documents stored in the Clitheroe museum building. Two high-quality full-size photographic copies are now in the Clitheroe reference library.

The argument about where old written documents and drawings should be kept is an ongoing one. One school of thought wishes all material to be kept locally; the second wishes it to be placed in a central and closely supervised environment, e.g. a record office. It is not the purpose of this article to argue the pros and cons – there are many – on each side. A useful working compromise would be to ensure that good copies of some documents are available within the locality. Certainly the present storage facilities, on the top floor of the museum where there are problems of dampness and humidity, are inadequate by modern standards of preservation.

As far as can be ascertained, the two sketches have only been reproduced, much smaller than their original size, in two booklets by David Best:

Nov 1988 – *A Short History of Clitheroe*
1990 – *Clitheroe Castle*

In the first publication it is suggested that the artist was George Vertue. This artist, publisher, engraver and antiquarian was responsible for the 1753 sketch of Clitheroe, itself based on a late sixteenth-century drawing – see earlier essay. George Vertue died in 1756 aged 72 years.

The Keep 1848 – (1) Ruinous State

The Keep August 1848 – (2) What restoration might do.

The sketches are important because they are the only known detailed drawings of the keep made before the days of photography. It is very unlikely that Arthur Langshaw, Clitheroe's major local historian, saw them. He would assuredly have made a reference to them.

Their significance is twofold. One sketch shows the ruinous state of the keep, particularly the north-east and north-west exterior walls. The second drawing indicates what should be done to restore the keep to a safe condition.

It is evident from the first sketch that the north-east wall needed a tremendous amount of repair to make it as we see it today and as it would have looked in Norman times. Stonework has disappeared from the entrance on the first floor right to the ground. The base of the north-east corner has almost gone. The south-west corner has been badly damaged and eroded with the help of the elements and of man. Only the north-west corner – the strongest of the four corners – is relatively unscathed.

This is the corner which has winding steps leading to the third floor and eventually to the battlements. Reference has been made, in the first article, to the inconclusive evidence regarding the slighting of the castle. The sketch does offer an arguable case for what may have been attempted.

The second sketch showing suggestions for repair was indeed the basis of what was done. The two archways leading to the main room in the keep are as we see them today, as is the lower archway leading through into what was the storage room.

Also very much in evidence are the buttresses we see 150 years later. No known records exist showing exactly when or how much was spent in repairing the keep. It seems reasonable to assume that once a decision had been made to repair, it would have been done promptly.

In 1884 George T. Clarke wrote in *Medieval Military Architecture in England*:

"All is neatly kept, and is in as substantial repair as becomes a ruin; but his Grace's most commendable zeal does certainly obscure the fabric it preserves, and it is to be rgretted that the new work was not made more clearly distinguishable from the old."

Local historians are given to conjecture. It is very tempting to say, "Why draw only two exterior walls?" It is quite sensible to argue that all four walls were sketched. Perhaps the missing drawings will turn up in the 21st century.

It is relevant to mention the two mill chimneys shown on the first sketch. If we stand as closely as possible at the point from which the artist was working, the larger chimney can only be that of Salford Mill or Holmes Mill. The latter, known locally as Thornbers for almost a century and the only surviving mill in the town, is still run by the Thornber family. The smaller chimney in the far distance could belong to Primrose Mill. How intriguing to have a sketch showing what, at that time, was still a Norman construction together with evidence of Clitheroe's emergence as a nineteenth-century cotton town.

Clitheroe's Honour –
Divided, Limited, Sold

I T is important to make some comment on the Honour of Clitheroe during the eighteenth and nineteenth centuries. This may have a bearing on why the sketches were drawn in 1848.

When John, 2nd Duke of Montague, died in 1749 only two of his children survived him, Isabella and Mary. The Honour was divided between them. Confirmation of this is at Lancashire Record Office, where papers belonging to the Parkers of Browsholme are held. An agreement dated 1770 endorses the appointment of a Steward to the Honour agreed by Edward, Lord Beaulieu, Isabella his wife, George Duke of Montague (recreated in 1766) and his wife Mary.

Both husbands died before their wives and only Elizabeth, a daughter of Mary, was left to inherit her Aunt Isabella's share and her mother's share. As there was no son left to inherit, the recreated title of Duke of Montague lapsed when George died in 1790. His family name, Brudenell is linked with the title, Earl of Cardigan, hence the Cardigan Avenue as well as De Lacy Street, Albemarle Street, Montague Street and Buccleuch Avenue.

Note from the family tree that the Buccleuch link does not begin until Elizabeth, granddaughter of John inherits after the deaths of her aunt and mother. It is interesting to note the political/child marriage of the first Buccleuchs at the ages of 14 and 12. In national history books, of course, the first Duke is better known as Duke of Monmouth, beheaded in 1685. He was a son of Charles II.

So from 1749 to 1827 the Honour of Clitheroe was passed down through the female side of the Montagues and Buccleuchs. We need to bear in mind the high infant and adult mortality rates even amongst the aristocracy. Elizabeth outlived her husband and her eldest son Charles, the 4th Duke.

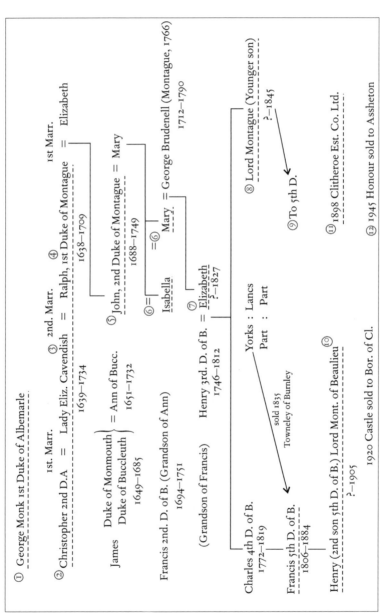

① George Monk 1st Duke of Albemarle

② Christopher 2nd D.A = Lady Eliz. Cavendish
1st Marr.
1639–1734

③ Ralph, 1st Duke of Montague = Elizabeth
2nd. Marr. 1st Marr.
1638–1709

④

James   Duke of Monmouth = Ann of Bucc.
Duke of Buccleuth
1649–1685   1651–1732

⑤ John, 2nd Duke of Montague = Mary
1688–1749

Francis 2nd. D. of B. (Grandson of Ann)
1694–1751

⑥=   =⑥
Isabella   Mary = George Brudenell (Montague, 1766)
1712–1790

(Grandson of Francis)

⑦
Henry 3rd. D. of B. = Elizabeth
1746–1812   ?–1827

Yorks : Lancs
Part : Part

⑧ Lord Montague (Younger son)
?–1845

⑨ To 5th D.

sold 1835
Towneley of Burnley

Charles 4th D. of B.
1772–1819

Francis 5th D. of B.
1806–1884

⑩
Henry (2nd son 5th D. of B.) Lord Mont. of Beaulieu
?–1905

1920 Castle sold to Bor. of Cl.

⑪ 1898 Clitheroe Est. Co. Ltd.

⑫ 1945 Honour sold to Assheton

Holders of The Honour of Clitheroe from 1661

On her death in 1827 Elizabeth willed the Yorkshire part of the Honour to her grandson, the 5th Duke of Buccleuch (1806–1884). The Lancashire part she left to a younger son, Lord Montague. He died in 1845 without a son – he had four daughters. The Lancashire part of the Honour reverted to his nephew, the 5th Duke. We are reminded of the plot in Jane Austen's *Pride and Prejudice*. Mr Bennet had five daughters. His estate was entailed and Mr Collins, the obsequious clergyman, was due to inherit on the death of Mr Bennet.

Meanwhile, in 1835, the Duke sold the Yorkshire part of the Honour which came to him in 1827. It became the property of a local family, the Towneleys of Burnley. What about the Lancashire part which, of course, included Clitheroe Castle? What incentive had Lord Montague to spend money on repairing the keep when the property went to a nephew who had already disposed of the part left to him?

How did the 5th Duke feel when the Lancashire part became his after the death of his uncle? Did he feel guilty about selling the Yorkshire part? Probably not. Did he visit Clitheroe and talk to his Steward, Dixon Robinson appointed in the 1830s? How much influence did Dixon Robinson have? He is listed in an 1824 directory as a solicitor in Clitheroe. He held the post as Steward until his death in 1878. A son and grandson continued the tradition.

When the 5th Duke died in 1884 the Honour passed to his second son, Lord Montague of Beaulieu. During his tenure various members of the family became trustees of Clitheroe Estates Co. Limited. This company owned the Honour. It was formed in 1898. It sold the castle and grounds to the Borough of Clitheroe in November 1920 and eventually sold the Honour to the Assheton family of Downham in 1945 in whose hands it still remains.

N.B. In 1939 the Towneley Family sold their part of the Honour to the Duchy of Lancaster, i.e. the Crown. The visit of The Queen to Dunsop Bridge in 1989 celebrated the 50th anniversary of the 1939 event.

Castlegate

THIS essay examines briefly changes which occurred close to the castle itself, mainly in the approaches to it. Castlegate is a name which has very largely superseded an older and now rarely used name of Castle Foot. Oddie has drawn some of the properties which existed in the area; they are at the extreme right of the picture.

Firstly remember that Moor Lane was not built until 1809. Property had to be demolished at 'X' as I have indicated on the 1822 map. 'Z' was the Red Lion Inn, called Crosskeys in the late eighteenth century. By 1849 it too had been demolished to widen the approach into Castle Street. It was rebuilt at 'Z', and survived as an inn until the early 1960s.

Area 'C' was developed after 1810 and until the 1860s was occupied by the New Black Bull, together with its stables and outhouses. Subsequently, with alterations and different types of occupiers the site has been used for many years by the Midland Bank and Steele and Son, Solicitors. The Ordnance Survey of 1912 is the first to show a bank on the site.

In June 1834 some 65 lots of land and property within Clitheroe were auctioned at the Swan (and Royal). Lord Howe, a major landowner, a member of the Curzon family, was getting rid of his Clitheroe interests. The need to retain ownership had disappeared two years earlier with the passing of the 1832 Reform Bill. Until then the town, a pocket borough, returned two M.P.s. The Curzon family provided one through voting rights exercised by owner-ship of key properties. After 1832 the town had one M.P., individual voters had more influence though it was not until 1872 that they were able to vote in secret. A number of election records exist showing how people voted, either Tory or Whig and later Conservative or Liberal.

The selling of property happened throughout the country where wealthy landowners had accrued voting rights. It also explains why a great deal of

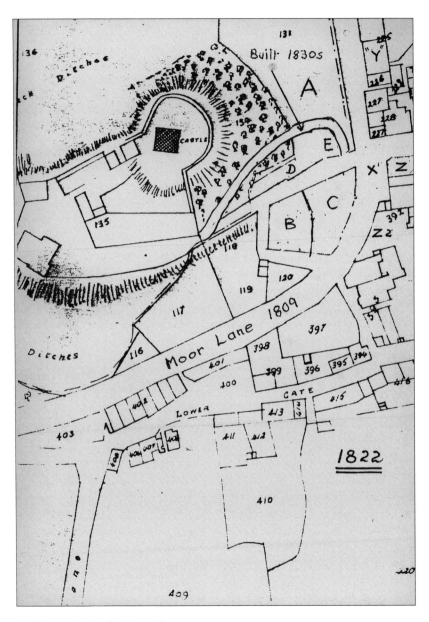

Castlegate Area in the nineteenth century.

Castle Street was bought by various purchasers and redeveloped in the late 1830s right through into the 1860s.

Area 'B' was Lot 46, described below, as is Area 'A' Lot 47.

Lot 46

All that small shop and dwelling house, situate at Castle Foot, and three cottages adjoining, with yards and gardens behind the same, as described in the plan, the whole containing 570 square yards, more or less, in the several occupations of Ellen Sellers, Ed Astley, George Fielding and the Overseers of the poor of Clitheroe.

Lot 47

All that cottage, barn and shippon, situate on the west side of Castle Foot, containing 270 square yards, more or less, together with a valuble piece of building land, called Cliff Croft situate on the south side of the Lancaster Road, containing 3,700 square yards, more or less, as described in the plan, in the occupation of George Slater, Matthew Standen and Thomas Carr Esq.

Lot 47 is the more interesting of the two. This was glebe land, the income from which went towards the living of a clergyman. Amongst the 1834 conditions of sale is a reference to various deeds going back to 1547 regarding payments of rents and other dues involving the Archbishop of Canterbury and the Crown. Further reference is made to the fact that the financial interests in these matters had been recently sold to Thomas Carr, solicitor and Steward of the Honour of Clitheroe. Surprise, Surprise! The sale plan shows that permission had already been given for a new driveway to be constructed to the castle.

Within ten years the old properties had been demolished and the three new cottages D built together with a large lodge house E by the new entrance to the castle. Paintings and photographs of these properties have long been favourite shots for pictures in the homes of many Clitheronians. The lodge and cottages survived until after the Second World War when they were demolished to enable the present castle entrance to be built. Thomas Carr had bought at least three other lots of land close to the castle boundary.

In August 1936 the *Advertiser and Times* published information provided

Castlegate – the three cottages 'D' and lodge house 'E'. Built in the 1840s, demolished late 1940s.

by Arthur Langshaw. This stated that Lot 47, i.e. the glebe land, was farmed by Rev. T. Wilson, Headmaster of the Grammar School and Vicar of Clitheroe. He lived at Cliffes, a house which stood where lodge house 'E' was built. In his book Clitheroe's Thousand Years, Langshaw indicates that Mr Wilson's house was at 'Y' the site of the present Surbiton House in Parson Lane. As Thomas Wilson lived in the town 38 years (1775–1813) it is quite feasible that he lived for a time at each of these sites.

The Castle Jigsaw – Final Pieces?

Two earlier chapters, 'The 'New' Castle' and 'The Keep – Saved by an Unknown Artist', discussed in some depth the significance of the M. Oddie 1781 sketch and the Castle Keep sketches of 1848.

The recent discovery of these drawings has continued to give added impetus to further investigation which has resulted in further definite information coming to light. Rather than re-write what has been noted in these two chapters – both still relevant – I thought it more informative to show, in this final chapter, how local history is an ongoing process.

Each generation of local historians follows two basic paths:

(a) returning to familiar information – often missed or disregarded as un-important at the first or earlier readings

(b) looking for material previously not known about e.g. M. Oddie sketch.

In this last chapter I have made much use of research work undertaken by Mr Cyril Ainsworth into the accounts for the castle and Steward's house. During the last twenty years Cyril Ainsworth has taken on the mantle of Arthur Langshaw and Henry Forrest. Few residents of Clitheroe will realise how much painstaking work he has done in classifying and indexing local history materials. He has shared his expertise and knowledge with many organisations and individuals who are interested in Clitheroe's past. Clitheroe reference library has benefited a great deal from his efforts and the staff there have been quick to realise the value of his work and in their turn have been able to offer the public an excellent, friendly service. I have been very pleased to have had Cyril's support and friendship in recent years.

The 4th updated and corrected edition of Whitaker's *History of Whalley Parish* is the most useful one for local historians interested in Clitheroe. Published in 1876, it contains many footnotes and it is in these notes that details are tucked away regarding the castle in the 1840s. On page 69 of Volume II the following is disclosed:

Re Keep   The lower portion, however was refaced in limestone and underwent a substantial process of reparation in 1849–50.

Re Mansion It is believed that this house was erected about the middle of the eighteenth century. Considerable alterations were carried out in 1849–50 by Mr. Little, architect, of London who also at this time superintended the restoration of the Keep. A few years later the walls of the old courthouse were refaced, the mullioned windows restored and a new Tudor doorway was built.

Confirmation of this comes from detailed listing below:

Items from Stewards' Accounts in the Honor of Clitheroe for the Castle and Steward's House only

Ref. Lancs. Record Office DDHC1

Early Accounts were rendered from Michaelmas to Michaelmas.

1848 by cash paid for stone mason's work done in repairing the Norman Keep at C. C. according to a design prepared by Mr Little, and for Stones, Lime, Sand, Cement and other materials used in such repairs and for scaffolding used on the occasion and valued by Mr Thomas Chaffer, Builder Burnley and afterwards examined and approved by Mr Little.

172   3   2

The paragraph confirms Mr. Little as designer and gives a cost of £172 3*s.* 2*d.*, inclusive of labour and materials. The paragraph below pinpoints further work to the Flag Tower and staircase in 1853.

1853 paid to Messrs Lawrence Robinson and Brother, stone masons, for work done and materials provided by them in the Summer of 1853 in repairing the Flag Tower in the North corner of the ancient Keep at C.C. according to the design of Mr Little and restoring the Winding Stone Staircase which had become ruinous and in a dangerous state.

49   13   10

So has the unknown artist of the 1848 Keep sketches been found? It seems reasonable to argue that they were drawn by Mr. Little, the London architect employed by the 5th Duke of Buccleuch. We have a Burnley builder carrying out the instructions of a London architect to save Clitheroe's most notable feature! Nothing new here. Clitheroe has often made great use of outsiders who have influenced and/or chronicled the town's development:

☐ Jeremiah Garnett, 1775–1853, responsible for Low Moor Mill from 1799;

☐ James Thomson, a highly regarded industrial chemist and textile engineer responsible for Primrose Print Works from 1810 to 1850;

☐ three town clerks, who spanned almost one hundred years in office, Robert Trappes from Knaresborough, 1836–1862, John Eastham from Mitton 1862–1909, William Self Weeks from Isle of Wight 1909–1935;

☐ Stephen Clarke, local historian from Skipton area, 1854–1924;

☐ Arthur Langshaw local historian from Whalley 1880–1952;

☐ John O Neil from Carlisle, writer of the Low Moor Diaries 1810–1876;

☐ Eli Tucker Somerset 1841–1926 who for fifty years operated a popular boating business at Brungerley Bridge.

Bearing in mind the fact that the Duke inherited the Lancashire part of the Honor of Clitheroe from his uncle in 1845 it is evident a decision was quickly made to spend a considerable amount of the Steward's House and grounds:

1850 by work done at C. c. in the years 1849 and 1850
      as reported by Mr Little, the Architect viz.

General repairs	72	67	0
Fire Proof Record Room	73	0	0
Alteration and Additions to the House	440	14	0
	124	01	0
Bell Hanging and Gas Fittings	45	0	0
	1285	1	0
additional works as per account January 1851	234	8	6
	1519	9	6

1855 by cash for the Green House and Terrace on the
      south side of the House at C. C. as per statement
      and particulars sent herewith   232   19   9

48

The New Castle — Steward's House — Museum since 1980s

The earliest Steward's accounts of the eighteenth century yet found date from
August 1742. The information given is vital. I am seeking to persuade the
reader that the evidence provided narrows the time scale of when the house
was built from the (doubtful) 1723 precise date given by Arthur Langshaw
and the vague term, middle of the eighteenth century given by most other
writers.

1742

27 Aug paid Edward [Anson] for the freight of 226 feet of
Deal Balk from Liverpool to Preston | 1 | 0 | 9
1 Oct paid Roger Kenyon, nailor, for nails | 4 | 10 | 1
29 Oct paid John Ecroyd for 504 feet of glass at 5*d* per
foot | 10 | 10 | 0
20 Nov paid Richard Broughton, mason, for [hewing] and
walling Battlement and other work | 39 | 13 | 9
30 Dec paid William Hayhurst, plumer, and glazier for
pluming work at Clitheroe Castle | 39 | 2 | 7
1743/44 total expenditure was | 76 | 8 | 4¾

I suggest that the detailed evidence indicates that the building project was
into its final stages during the autumn of 1742, i.e. putting glass in window
frames and building the battlements. The frontage of the house entrance uses
approximately 240 sq. ft. of glass and another 260 sq. ft. would have completed
most of the windows in the rest of the house. Nearly £95 was spent in the
last four months of 1742 and a further £77 in 1743. The probable dating of
the building is therefore likely to be 1740–1743, certainly no later.

The Court House

1767/68 paid Thomas Drinkwater & another for Oak timber
intended to be used on new roofing said Court House
the next sumner | 31 | 2 | 0
1768/69 repairs to Court House at C.C. | 63 | 0 | 0
1769/70 paid Benjamin Smith, woodmonger, for 124 yards
of oak boards delivered at Nethertown near Whalley
and intended to be used in new flooring the Court

Another little known sketch of the Keep. c.1920, Artist Albert Woods, 1871–1944 – Preston Born

	House at Clithero Castle	8	13	6
	All are now in the Castle yard			
1770/71	repairs to Court House at C.C.	10	12	6
1773/74	The Record Room and Courthouse there intended to be repaired – paid to James Dewhurst for a hearth stone for the intended Record Room and flaggs for the Court House	11	6	0
1774/75	repairs to Court House and building Record Room	109	1	6
1775/76	repairs to Court House and Record Room	13	3	3
1779	for flagging the Court House paid John Roscow of Haslingden Grain for 73 yards of strong slabs brought from Hutch Bank near Haslingden	4	2	6
1781	paid John Riley of Gisburne for drawing and planning etc. at the Court House at C.C., in			

the years 1773 and 1774 and which has heretofore
by mistake   1   10   9

Closer examination of the accounts show that between 1767 and 1779 more than £243 was spent on updating and repairing this building, suggesting a gap of some twenty-five years between the building of the Stewards' House and renovation of the Court House.

It is interesting to have an independent assessment and comparison of costs. The Clitheroe Grammar School – rebuilt in 1781–1782 is an estimated one-third larger than the court house. The estimate for the rebuilding of the school was £375, the final cost £420.

Castle Walls

The extract below, 1843, refers to the section of the wall now seen at the rear of Steele's the solicitors where the stone gateway can be seen in the wall itself (mentioned in a previous chapter 'The 'New' Castle'). This was a more costly operation than the repair to the Keep.

1843 by cash to William Hargreaves & Co, stone masons, the account of their bill for erecting a wall along part of the East, North and West boundaries of the Castle.

Ditches, the old wall of the East side being partly undermined and in a very dangerous and delapidated state in consequence of the rock being got by the proprietors of the adjoining land and the new wall being required in one part to be eight yards high on the outside altho' only five feet on the inside and for Sundry other repairs to the Castle

213   14   9

The major items of expenditure discussed above are further put in perspective in so far that the accounts show that an additional £700 was spent in the one hundred years between 1743 and 1843 in the general maintenance of all buildings and boundary walls of Clitheroe Castle. This included a sum of £32 18s. 8d. for re-roofing and slating the stables and cart house in 1780.

Postscript – A Secret Revealed

THE emphasis in this book has been on the castle. It seems appropriate to end by revealing a well-kept secret between myself and the late Coun. Jimmy Fell of Whalley.

For older and long-standing residents of the Ribble Valley he is remembered amongst many other things, for a lively, friendly and long running local history column in the *Clitheroe Advertiser and Times*. His contribution for 7 August 1980 follows:

> OUR old town of Clitheroe, a place for which I have a particular affection, holds much of which it can be proud. A delightful countryside, the knowledge that it was once the second oldest borough in the county, the fact that it is the administrative centre of the Ribble Valley Council.
>
> It can proudly boast, too, that its ancient castle, perched high on its limestone rock, is "the smallest Norman keep in the country." Or can it?
>
> Where I first heard the assertion that we owned the "smallest keep," I do not know. It is – was – a fraction of knowledge tucked away in my mind from my earliest days and I have seen it in print in a dozen or more guide books and similar publications.
>
> Indeed, I have written to that effect myself and publically asserted the same on numerous occasions. You will read it in "The walk through Clitheroe" compiled by the local Civic Society and published by the Ribble Valley Council, although Aurthur Langshaw in his "Child's history of Clitheroe" was slightly cautious and merely wrote — "it is said to be the smallest Norman keep in the country."
>
> Well, the Civic Society and numerous other compilers and authors, myself included, were wrong.
>
> For me, the myth was exploded recently when a letter arrived on the mat which now, and for all time, puts the matter beyond all dispute.
>
> My correspondent wrote to say that he had heard me speak on the history

of the castle when I made once more the oft-repeated claim.

Now, in the politest terms he told me that I was wrong. He went on to say that quite by accident he had come across a smaller Norman keep.

He had checked the measurements carefully, inside and out; had even bought the Ministry of Works scale plan where the details were confirmed.

Now, I believe, for the first time, the horrible truth is publically revealed.

Clitheroe's Norman keep is not the smallest in the country. It is, apparently, the second smallest.

And where is the smallest then? It is at Goodrich, a delightful village about six miles from Ross-on-Wye.

I had, of course, no reason to doubt my informant. But I just had to go and see for myself.

Goodrich Castle, a very splendid castle, well preserved by the Department of the Environment, dates from the twelfth century. It is well worth a visit and, if you venture that far, in the middle of the grey old walls you will find the smallest Norman keep in the country.

It measures 29ft 6ins square against Clitheroe's 34ft 2ins square. The internal measurements are 14ft 6ins and 17ft respectively.

Now, I am sure you are going to ask why, having acquired this information, did your correspondent not make it public on his return home?

To put it bluntly, he was scared; scared of the surging wrath of 11,000 Clitheronians. He likes the town, wishes to continue living there in peace and comfort, and so he kept silent.

"I have kept the news quiet," he wrote, "fearing for my life having lived here for 16 years only."

Well, "Fools rush in . . ." you know the old proverb, and so now, in the interest of historical accuracy, I reveal all.

The truth is out and bang go my chances at the next election!

And, if vengeful Clitheronians come seeking my blood with sword and sabre, I shall barricade myself in our Whalley Abbey.

Select Bibliography

Ainsworth, C., *A Prospect of Old Clitheroe. Index of Stewards – The Honour of Clitheroe*

Baines, *History of Lancashire*, 1868

Clarke G. T., *Medieval Military Architecture*, 1884

Clarke S., *Clitheroe in its Coaching and Railway Days*

Dobson, *Walks by the Ribble*, 1864

Edwards, B. J. N., *Clitheroe Castle Antiquarians Journal*, 1984

Green D. & Harwood K., *Queen Mary's Grammar School Clitheroe*, 1983

Langshaw A., *Child's History of Clitheroe*, 1938. *Collected Works*, 1946–1953

Self Weeks W., *Clitheroe Parish Records*

Whitaker, T. D., *History of Parish of Whalley and Honour of Clitheroe* (4th edn, 1872)

Best D. J., *A Short History of Clitheroe*, 1988. *Clitheroe Castle*, 1990

Colne Reference Library. *Registers of Births, Deaths, Marriages and Wills of Colne*

Dictionary of National Biography

Lancashire Record Office, *Records of Marsden Area*; eighteenth- and nineteenth-century Stewards' Accounts, *Honour of Clitheroe*.